TUNED IN

A Comprehensive Approach to Band Intonation

GW00401416

BRIAN BALMAGES AND ROBERT HERRINGS

Table of Contents

About This Book:

Good intonation is one of the most important foundations of music. This book includes a downloadable set of drones in every key. You can also use your own electronic drone generated from a capable tuner or mobile app. Playing with drones helps musicians better understand pitch tendencies and further develops the ear. It is also important to play without drones, but always check your pitch with a tuner. Be sure to use both approaches as part of a regular practice routine. As with anything, the more you practice, the better your intonation will be!

 A speaker icon is included on lines that have a downloadable drone option, or musicians can use their own device to create a drone.

To access the free downloadable drones, visit **www.fjhmusic.com/downloads** and enter the following authentication code.

Website: **www.fjhmusic.com/downloads**
Authentication Code: 22283444142

CONCERT B♭ MAJOR / G MINOR

1. Chromatic Intervals
Play in any combination. A suggested progression is:
• Line A alone with recorded drone. • Line B alone with recorded drone.
• Line A and B combined with drone. • A, B and C combined (with and without recorded drone).

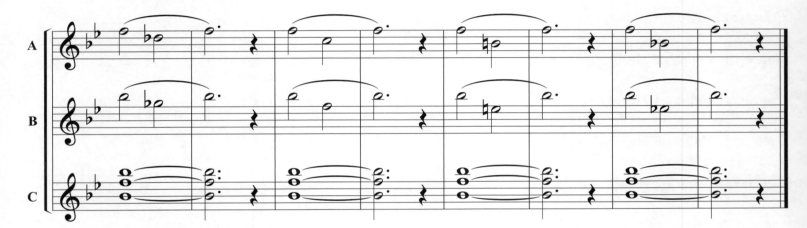

2. Interval Tuning
Play with recorded drone, then without.

3. Isolating Concert B♭
Play with recorded drone, then without.

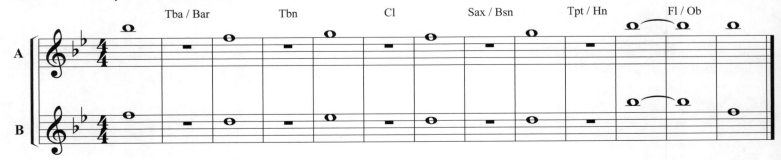

4. Chorale

Play using the following combinations:
- *With recorded drone.*
- *Without recorded drone, having various band members droning on concert B♭ and F.*
- *Chorale alone (without any drone).*

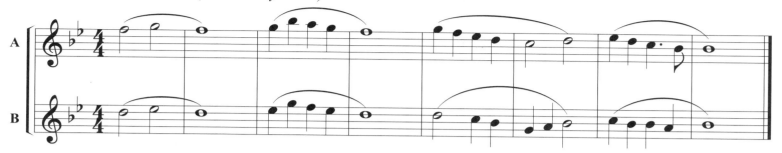

5. Concert G Minor Drone

Play with recorded drone, then without.

6. Descending Triads

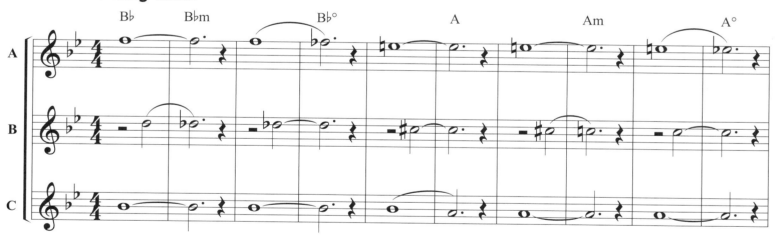

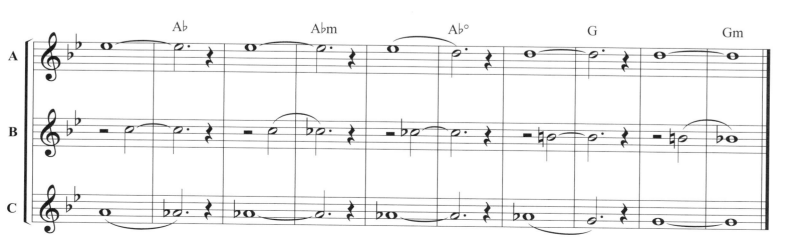

BB212FL

CONCERT E♭ MAJOR / C MINOR

1. Chromatic Intervals

Play in any combination. A suggested progression is:
- *Line A alone with recorded drone.* • *Line B alone with recorded drone.*
- *Line A and B combined with drone.* • *A, B and C combined (with and without recorded drone).*

2. Interval Tuning

Play with recorded drone, then without.

3. Isolating Concert E♭

Play with recorded drone, then without.

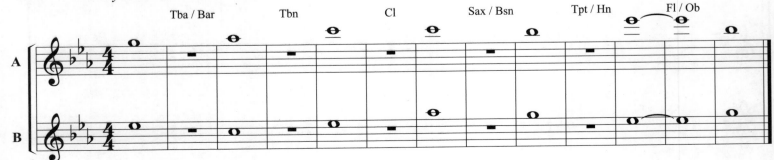

4. Chorale

Play using the following combinations:
- *With recorded drone.*
- *Without recorded drone, having various band members droning on concert E♭.*
- *Chorale alone (without any drone).*

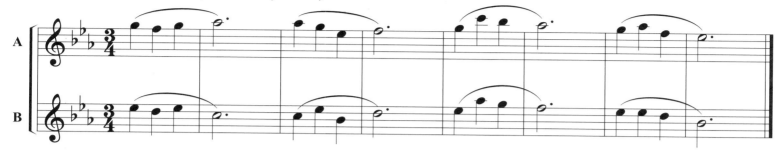

5. Concert C Minor Drone

Play with recorded drone, then without.

6. Descending Triads

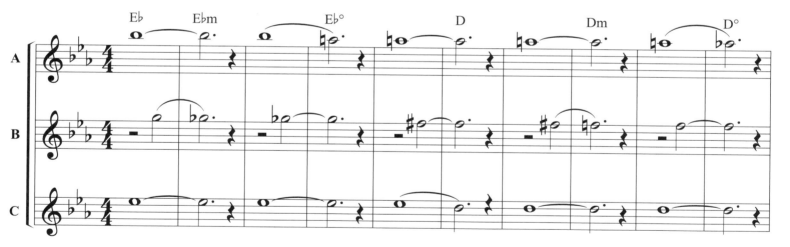

CONCERT F MAJOR / D MINOR

1. Chromatic Intervals

Play in any combination. A suggested progression is:
- *Line A alone with recorded drone.* • *Line B alone with recorded drone.*
- *Line A and B combined with drone.* • *A, B and C combined (with and without recorded drone).*

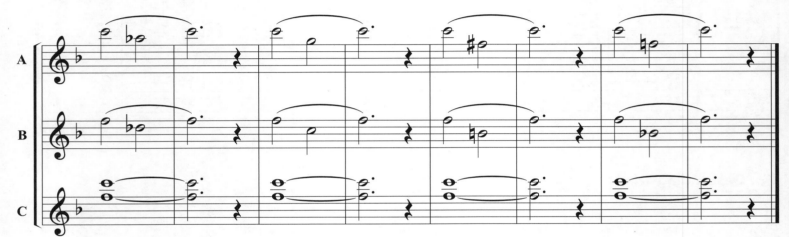

2. Interval Tuning

Play with recorded drone, then without.

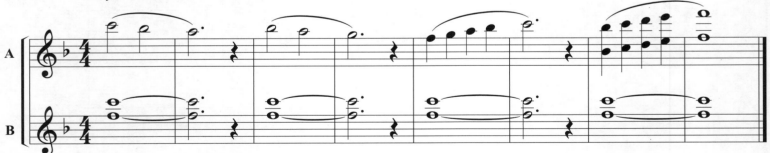

3. Isolating Concert F

Play with recorded drone, then without.

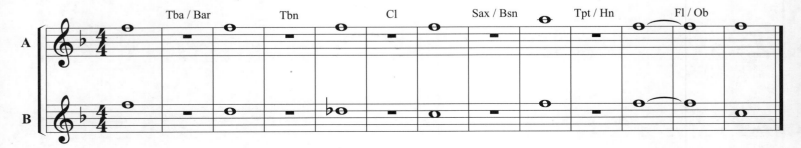

4. Chorale

Play using the following combinations:
- *With recorded drone.*
- *Without recorded drone, having various band members droning on concert F.*
  To further develop aural skills, add a concert C to the drone.
- *Chorale alone (without any drone).*

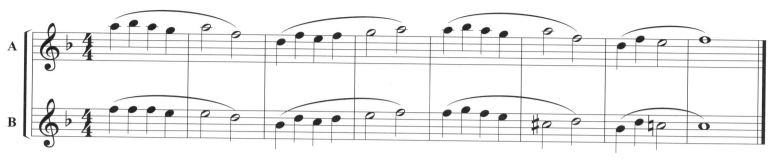

5. Concert D Minor Drone

Play with recorded drone, then without.

6. Descending Triads

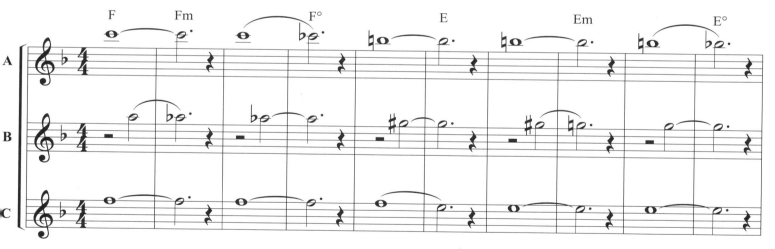

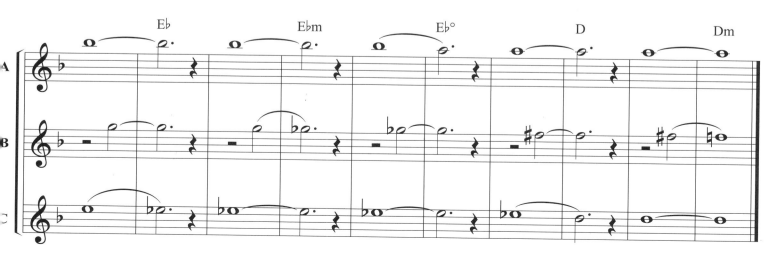

CONCERT C MAJOR / A MINOR

1. Chromatic Intervals

Play in any combination. A suggested progression is:
- *Line A alone with recorded drone.* • *Line B alone with recorded drone.*
- *Line A and B combined with drone.* • *A, B and C combined (with and without recorded drone).*

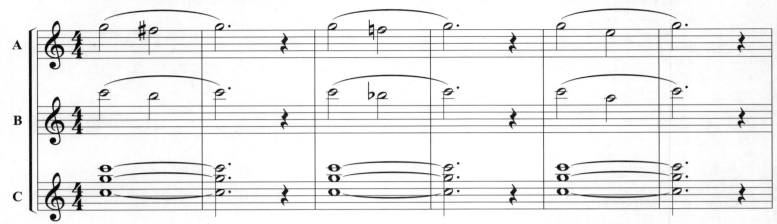

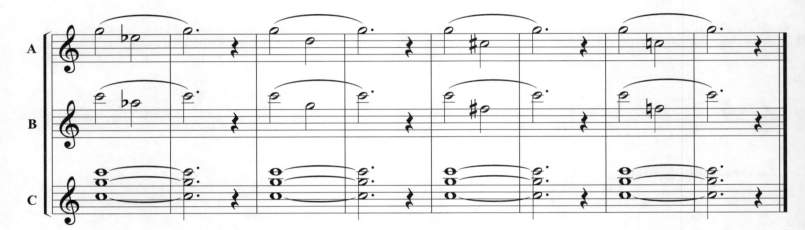

2. Interval Tuning

Play with recorded drone, then without.

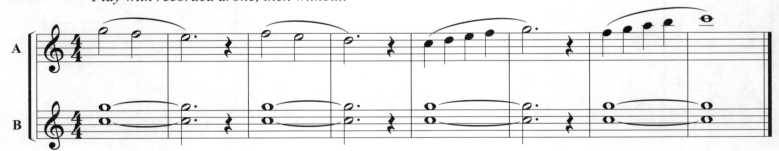

3. Isolating Concert C

Play with recorded drone, then without.

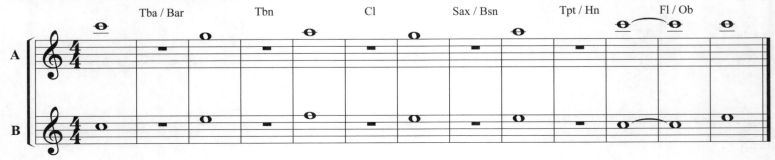

4. Chorale

Play using the following combinations:
- *With recorded drone.*
- *Without recorded drone, having various band members droning on concert C and G.*
- *Chorale alone (without any drone).*

5. Concert A Minor Drone

Play with recorded drone, then without.

6. Descending Triads

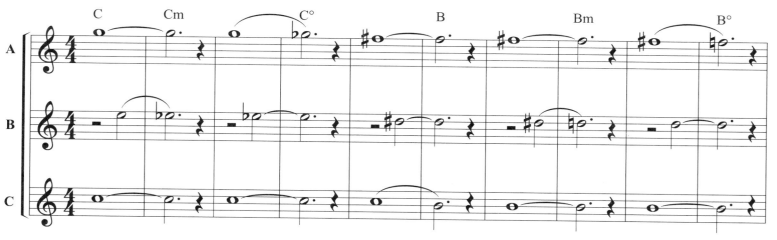

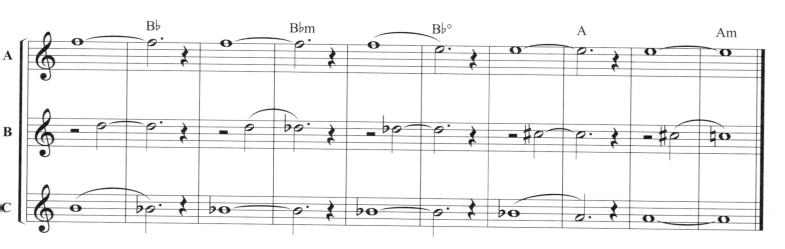

.BB212FL

CONCERT G MAJOR / E MINOR

1. Chromatic Intervals

Play in any combination. A suggested progression is:
- *Line A alone with recorded drone.* • *Line B alone with recorded drone.*
- *Line A and B combined with drone.* • *A, B and C combined (with and without recorded drone).*

2. Interval Tuning

Play with recorded drone, then without.

3. Isolating Concert G

Play with recorded drone, then without.

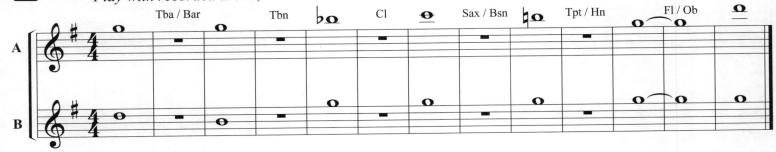

BB212FL

4. Chorale

Play using the following combinations:
- *With recorded drone.*
- *Without recorded drone, having various band members droning on concert G.*
  To further develop aural skills, add a concert D to the drone.
- *Chorale alone (without any drone).*

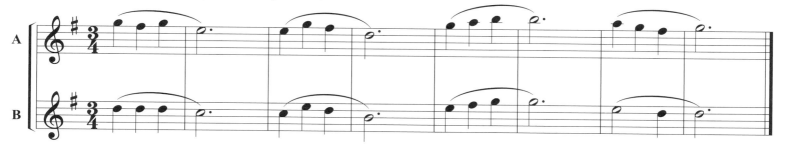

5. Concert E Minor Drone

Play with recorded drone, then without.

6. Descending Triads

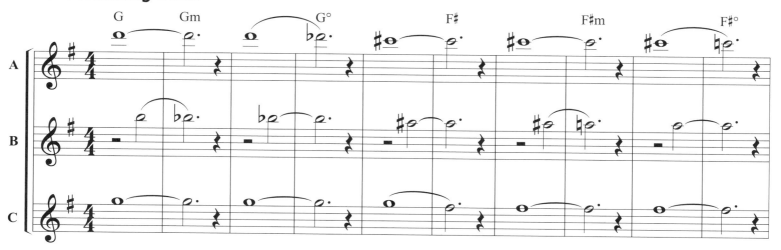

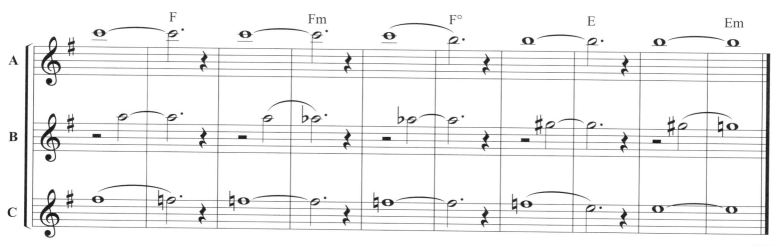

CONCERT D MAJOR / B MINOR

1. Chromatic Intervals

Play in any combination. A suggested progression is:
- *Line A alone with recorded drone.* • *Line B alone with recorded drone.*
- *Line A and B combined with drone.* • *A, B and C combined (with and without recorded drone).*

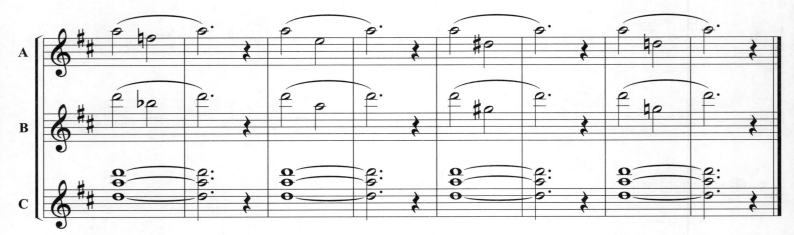

2. Interval Tuning

Play with recorded drone, then without.

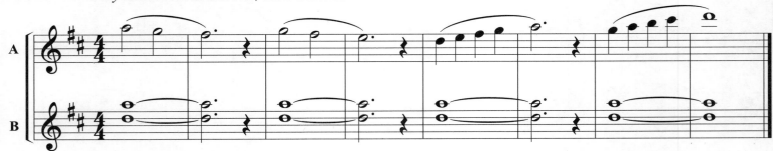

3. Isolating Concert D

Play with recorded drone, then without.

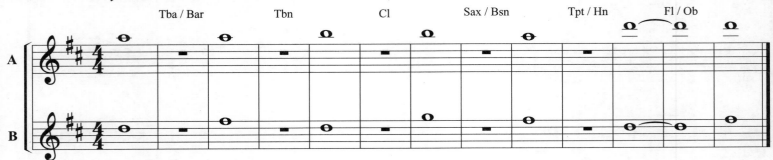

4. Chorale

In addition to playing the chorale alone, using a drone on concert D (recorded or played) will really stretch the ear in measure 4.

5. Concert B Minor Drone

Play with recorded drone, then without.

6. Descending Triads

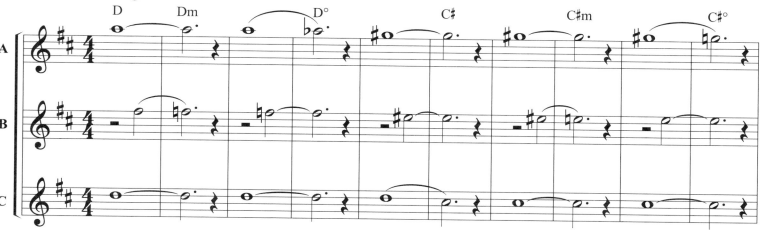

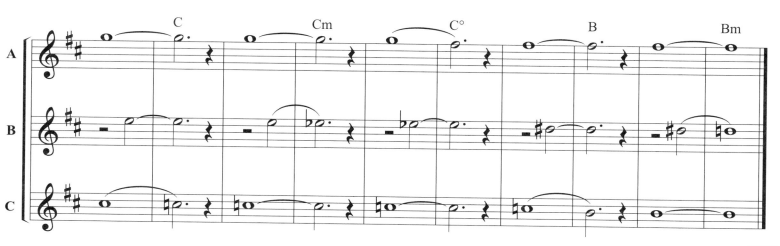

CONCERT A MAJOR / F♯ MINOR

1. Chromatic Intervals

Play in any combination. A suggested progression is:
- *Line A alone with recorded drone.* • *Line B alone with recorded drone.*
- *Line A and B combined with drone.* • *A, B and C combined (with and without recorded drone).*

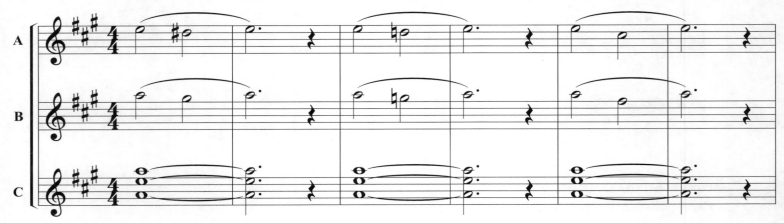

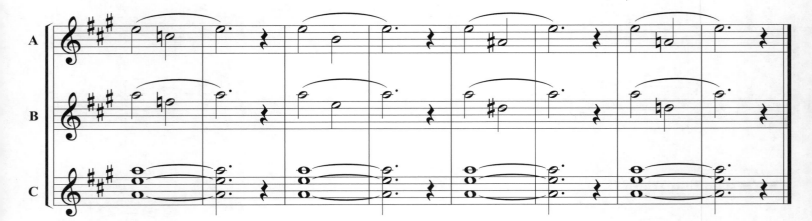

2. Interval Tuning

Play with recorded drone, then without.

3. Isolating Concert A

Play with recorded drone, then without.

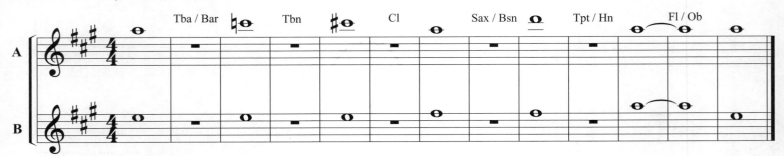

4. Chorale

Play using the following combinations:
- *With recorded drone.*
- *Without recorded drone, having various band members droning on concert A.*
  To further develop aural skills, add a concert E to the drone.
- *Chorale alone (without any drone).*

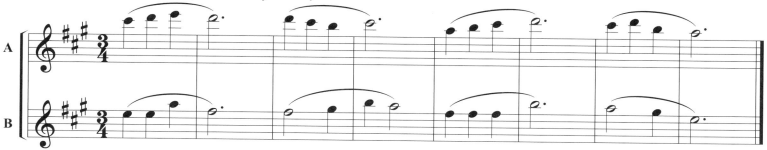

5. Concert F♯ Minor Drone

Play with recorded drone, then without.

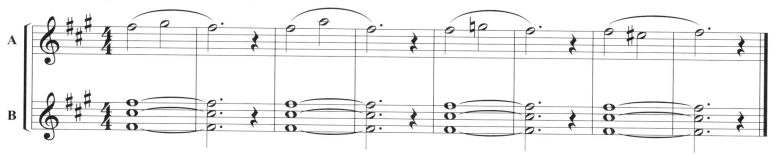

6. Descending Triads

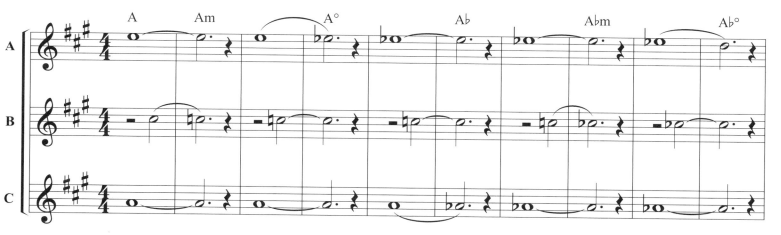

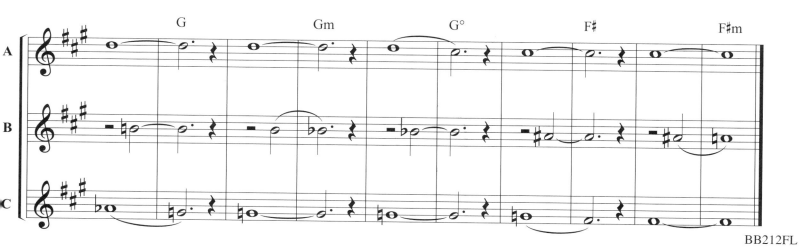

BB212FL

CONCERT E MAJOR / C# MINOR

1. Chromatic Intervals
Play in any combination. A suggested progression is:
- *Line A alone with recorded drone.* • *Line B alone with recorded drone.*
- *Line A and B combined with drone.* • *A, B and C combined (with and without recorded drone).*

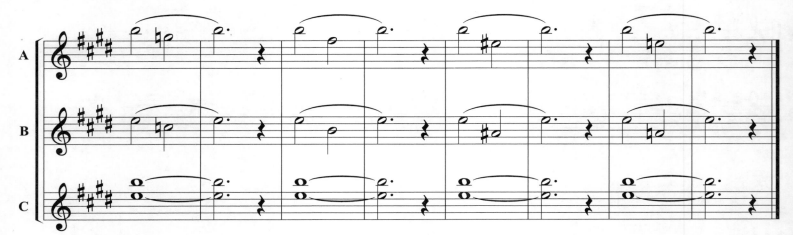

2. Interval Tuning
Play with recorded drone, then without.

3. Isolating Concert E
Play with recorded drone, then without.

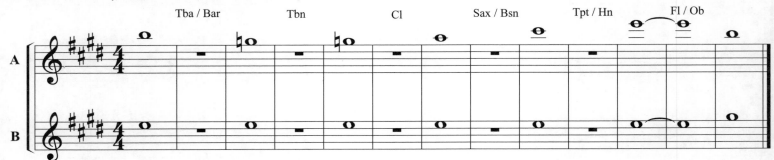

4. Chorale

Play using the following combinations:
- *With recorded drone.*
- *Without recorded drone, having various band members droning on concert E.*
- *Chorale alone (without any drone).*

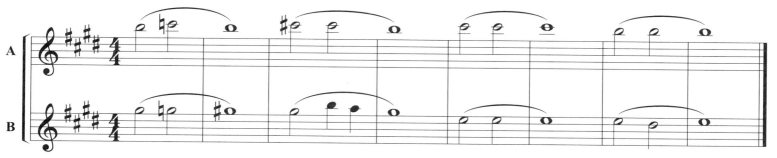

5. Concert C♯ Minor Drone

Play with recorded drone, then without.

6. Descending Triads

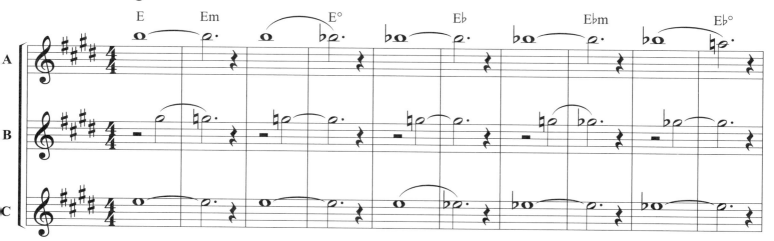

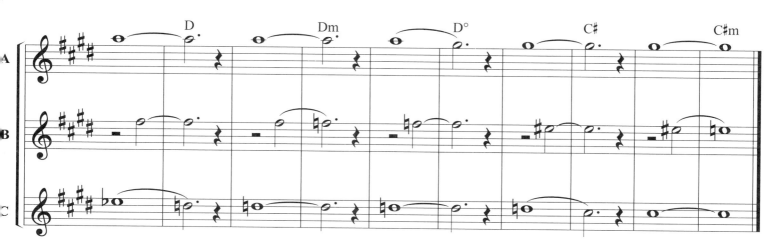

CONCERT B♭ MAJOR / G♯ MINOR

1. Chromatic Intervals

Play in any combination. A suggested progression is:
- *Line A alone with recorded drone.* • *Line B alone with recorded drone.*
- *Line A and B combined with drone.* • *A, B and C combined (with and without recorded drone).*

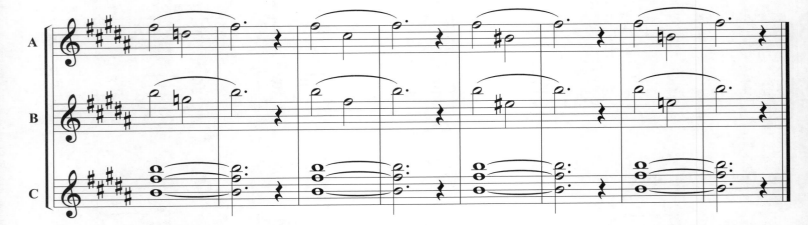

2. Interval Tuning

Play with recorded drone, then without.

3. Isolating Concert B♭

Play with recorded drone, then without.

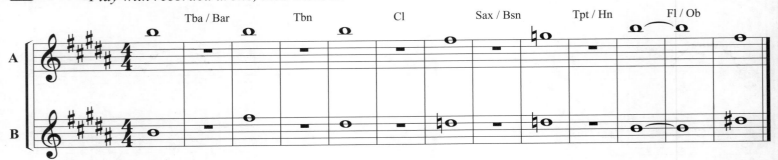

4. Chorale

Play using the following combinations:
- *With recorded drone.*
- *Without recorded drone, having various band members droning on concert B.*
    To further develop aural skills, add a concert F♯ to the drone.
- *Chorale alone (without any drone).*

5. Concert G♯ Minor Drone

Play with recorded drone, then without.

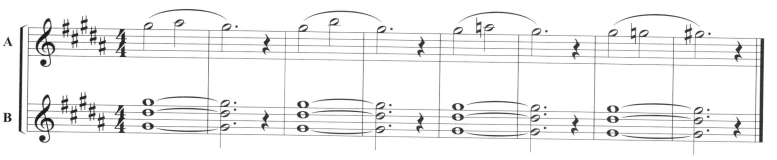

6. Descending Triads

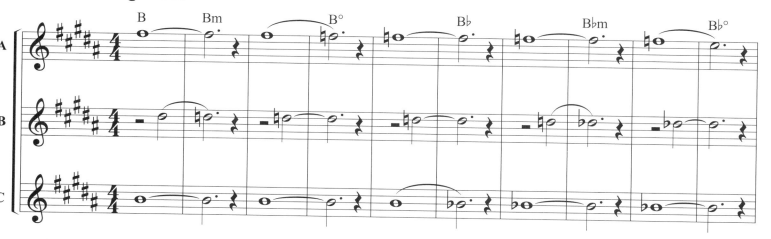

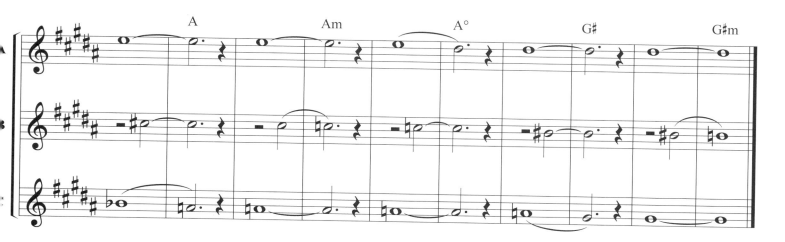

CONCERT G♭ MAJOR / E♭ MINOR

1. Chromatic Intervals

Play in any combination. A suggested progression is:
- *Line A alone with recorded drone.* • *Line B alone with recorded drone.*
- *Line A and B combined with drone.* • *A, B and C combined (with and without recorded drone).*

2. Interval Tuning

Play with recorded drone, then without.

3. Isolating Concert G♭

Play with recorded drone, then without.

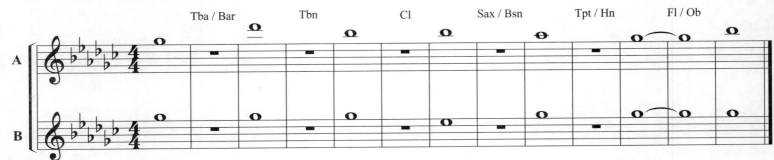

BB212FL

4. Chorale

Play using the following combinations:
- *With recorded drone.*
- *Without recorded drone, having various band members droning on concert G♭.*
    To further develop aural skills, add a concert D♭ to the drone.
- *Chorale alone (without any drone).*

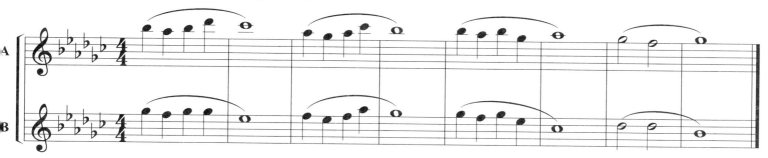

5. Concert E♭ Minor Drone

Play with recorded drone, then without.

6. Descending Triads

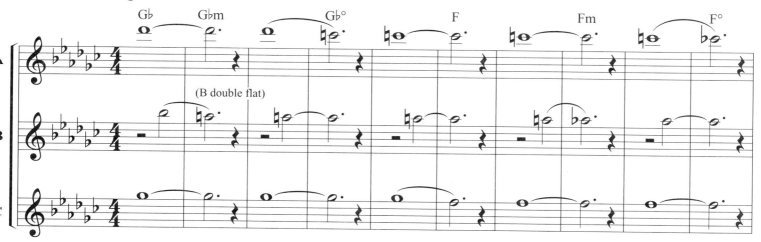

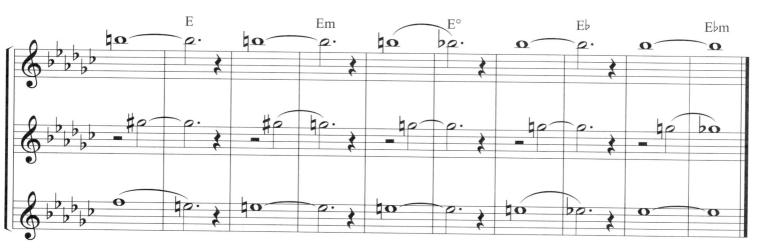

CONCERT D♭ MAJOR / B♭ MINOR

1. Chromatic Intervals

Play in any combination. A suggested progression is:
- *Line A alone with recorded drone.* • *Line B alone with recorded drone.*
- *Line A and B combined with drone.* • *A, B and C combined (with and without recorded drone).*

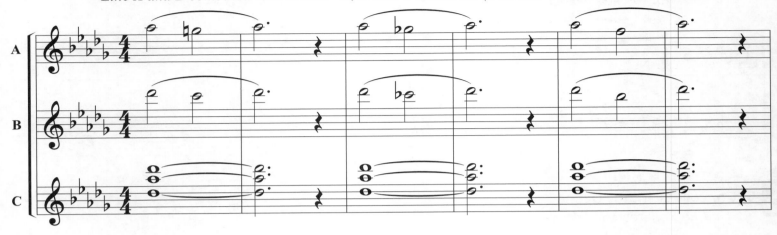

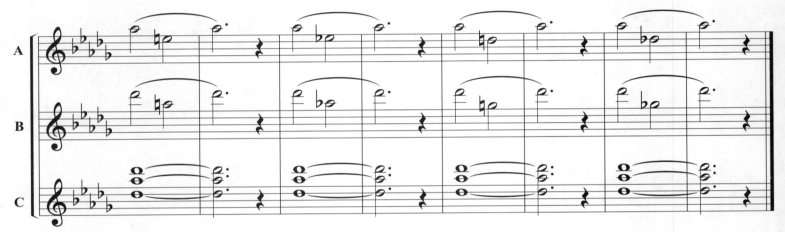

2. Interval Tuning

Play with recorded drone, then without.

3. Isolating Concert D♭

Play with recorded drone, then without.

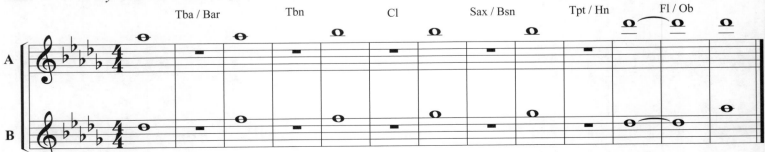

4. Chorale

Play using the following combinations:
- *With recorded drone.*
- *Without recorded drone, having various band members droning on concert D♭.*
  To further develop aural skills, add a concert A♭ to the drone.
- *Chorale alone (without any drone).*

5. Concert B♭ Minor Drone

Play with recorded drone, then without.

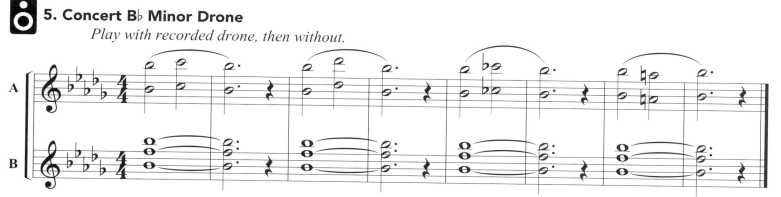

6. Descending Triads

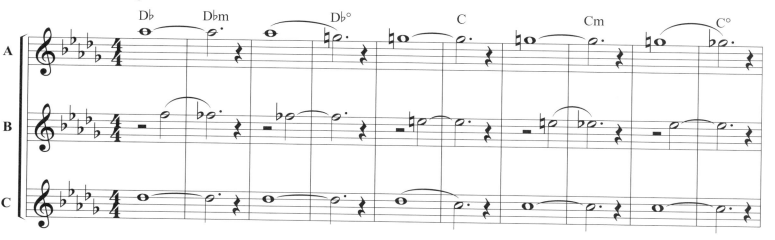

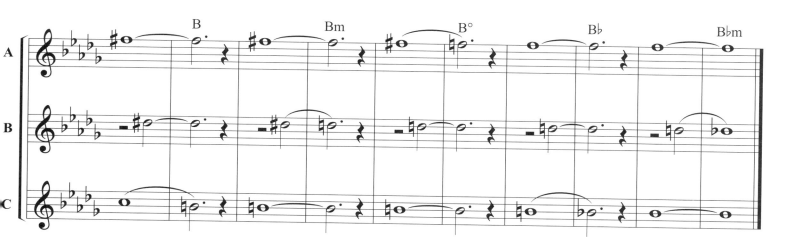

CONCERT A♭ MAJOR / F MINOR

1. Chromatic Intervals

Play in any combination. A suggested progression is:
• Line A alone with recorded drone. • Line B alone with recorded drone.
• Line A and B combined with drone. • A, B and C combined (with and without recorded drone).

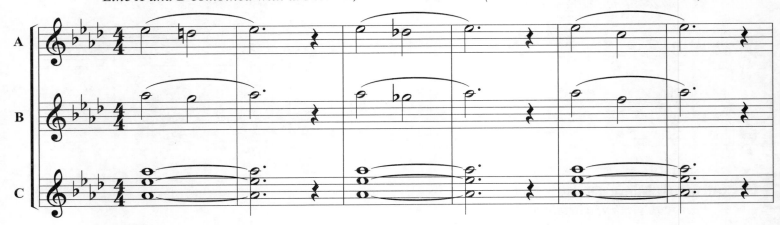

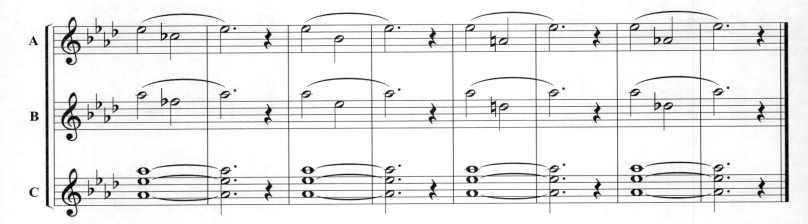

2. Interval Tuning

Play with recorded drone, then without.

3. Isolating Concert A♭

Play with recorded drone, then without.

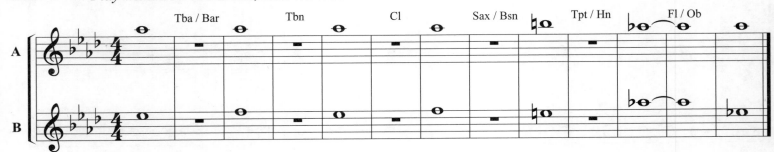

4. Chorale

Play using the following combinations:
- *With recorded drone.*
- *Without recorded drone, having various band members droning on concert A♭ and E♭.*
- *Chorale alone (without any drone).*

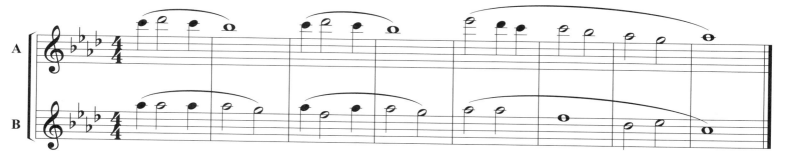

5. Concert F Minor Drone

Play with recorded drone, then without.

6. Descending Triads

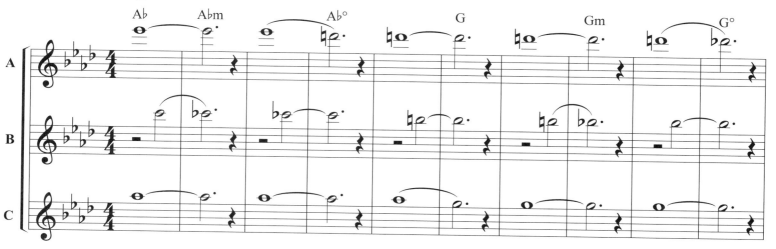

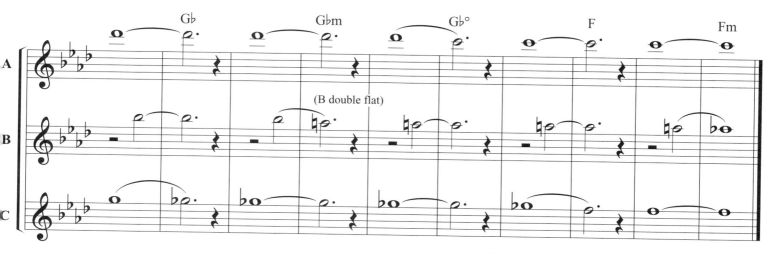

MAJOR AND MINOR SCALES

Play all scales with and without recorded drone. Suggested drone pitches are included for each scale.

Concert A Major

Concert A Minor

Concert E Major

Concert E Minor

Concert B Major

Concert B Minor

Concert Gb Major

Concert Gb (Concert F#) Minor

Concert Db Major

Concert Db (Concert C#) Minor

Concert Ab Major

Concert Ab Minor

12 CHORALES FOR BAND

BRIAN BALMAGES

Chorale No. 1 in B♭ Major

Chorale No. 2 in B♭ Major

Chorale No. 3 in G Minor

Chorale No. 4 in E♭ Major

Chorale No. 5 in E♭ Major

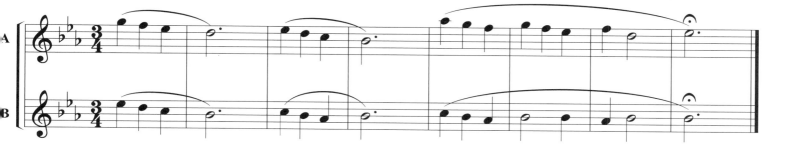

Chorale No. 6 in C Minor

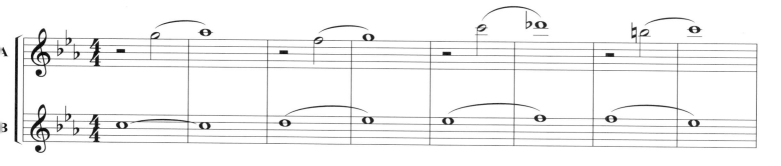

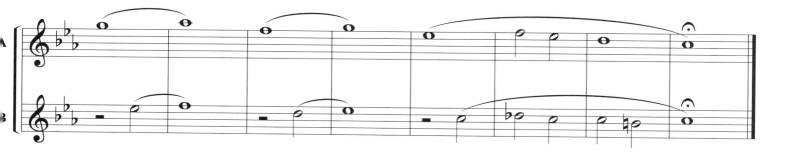

Chorale No. 7 in F Major

Chorale No. 8 in F Major

Chorale No. 9 in D Minor

Chorale No. 10 in A♭ Major

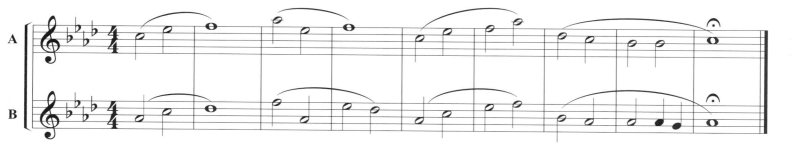

Chorale No. 11 in C Major

Chorale No. 12 in A Minor

WHOLE INSTRUMENT TUNING CHORALES

Multiple tuning notes are suggested under brackets for each instrument.
Tune each note to get an accurate snapshot of intonation.

Woodwind / Bass Tuning Notes and Chords

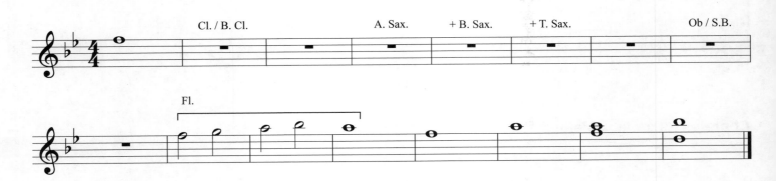

Full Band Comprehensive Tuning Chorale

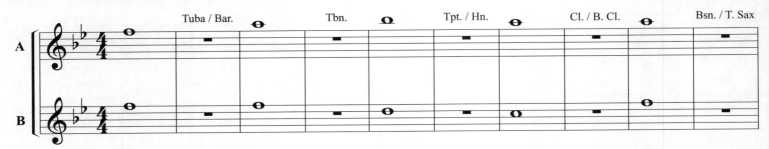

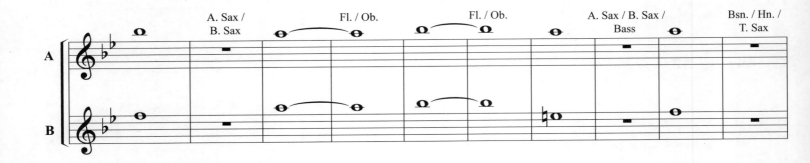

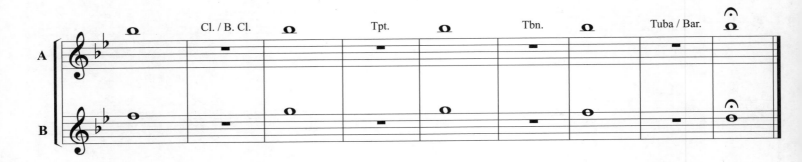